EXP

THE DEPTH OF
THE EXCHANGED LIFE

CHALLENGES IN
COMPLETING OBEDIENCE

Becky Castle

ISBN-13: 978-1727529951
ISBN-10: 1727529952

CONTENTS

PRINCIPLES OF EXCHANGING THE DEPTHS OF THE EXCHANGED LIFE

CHALLENGE ONE

Faith and belief in our position in Christ will always lead us to act as Jesus did.

CHALLENGE TWO

Crucifying the flesh is joining Christ on the cross, dying to our ideas, and relinquishing our right to live selfishly.

CHALLENGE THREE

Since the power of sin has been broken, a new authority has been given in our spirit to obey Christ.

CHALLENGE FOUR

You must make a choice to exchange this world with its passions and lusts, for living in the presence of God.

CHALLENGE FIVE

The grace of God creates an exchange in our life from death by enslavement to sin...to a life of obedience to Christ.

CHALLENGE SIX

Sin drains the vitality of the Spirit in the heart of the believer. Obedience is imperative for the filling of the Spirit.

CHALLENGE SEVEN

We must resist offering our minds to the thinking of this world and train our senses to obey God's truth.

CHALLENGE EIGHT

God's jealousy leaves no room for sharing of affections.

CHALLENGE NINE

Godly yieldedness brings a disposition of humility and grace to every situation.

CHALLENGE TEN

The exchanged life is marked by faith, love, and sacrifice.

OUR POSITION IN CHRIST'S KINGDOM

"Therefore, having been justified by faith, we have peace with our Lord Jesus Christ, through whom also we have obtained our introduction by faith into this grace in which we stand; and we exult in hope of the glory of God."

Romans 5:1-2

THE TRUTH REALIZED

Watchman Nee

God...made Him to sit...and made us to sit with Him....Christianity begins with not a big DO, but with a big DONE. The book of Ephesians opens with the statement that God has "Blessed us with every spiritual blessing in the heavenly places in Christ", and we are invited at the very outset to sit down and enjoy what God has done for us; not to set out and try to attain it for ourselves.... We begin our Christian life by depending not upon our own doing but upon what He had done. Until a man does this, he is no Christian; for to say, "I can do nothing to save myself; but by His grace God has done everything for me in Christ", is to take the first step in the life of faith. The Christian life from start to finish is based upon this principle of utter dependence upon the Lord Jesus.

Sit, Walk, Stand

EMBRACING THE TRUTH

A. The Transforming Life in Jesus Christ

Read Romans 3:21-28. What great miracle occurs in the life of one who believes in Christ?

_____

_____

What has happened to the old man, our body of sin? (Romans 6:6)

_____

_____

Our old nature was crucified with Christ. Not only have our sins been washed away, but our nature inclined toward sin has been rendered powerless. We are washed clean and made new by the indwelling Holy Spirit.

How do Ephesians 2:1-7 and Colossians 1:12-14 describe this transformation?

_____

_____

We have been taken out of darkness and death, to be placed in Christ and His kingdom – the kingdom of light and life.

What does 2 Corinthians 5:15, 17, 20-21 include in this exchange of life?

_____

_____

God is holy and perfect in everything He does. His power to accomplish His purposes is unlimited. By His Word, He holds all things together (Psalm 33:4-5, 9).

Because of who God is, what can we draw concerning the power of Jesus's death and resurrection to affect transformation in our life? (Romans 4:20-21)

_____

_____

God is fully able to do what He says. We can trust the promise of His Word to exchange Christ's life for ours, not just in Word but in actuality.

Read Ephesians 1:13-14. What changes have been made in your life because of the life of Christ?

_____

_____

_____

Through the blood of Jesus, our sins have been washed away. Through the cross, our old nature has been crucified. Through His resurrection, we who have believed in Him have been powerfully taken out of death and made alive unto God.

B. Tutored from Death to Life

Galatians 3:10-14 expresses that Christ redeemed us from the curse of the law by becoming a curse for us. What is the purpose of the law?

_____

_____

Unable to keep the law and attain a righteousness of his own, man is in need of the One who is able to do what he cannot.

The law of God acts as our personal tutor, leading us to Christ that "we might be justified by faith."

In what two ways is the exchange of His life for ours depicted? (Galatians 3:26-27)

_____

_____

Belief and trust in Jesus Christ makes us one with Him – He lives in us and we live in Him (Colossians 3:3). What is the result of this oneness with Christ? (Romans 7:4-6)

_____

_____

We can now obey in a new way by the transformation in our inward being. The One who now lives in us is able to obey and bear fruit for God in us (Romans 2:28-29). Since we are set free from the law, what is the ruling force of our relationship with God? (Romans 6:14)

_____

_____

Living in the grace of God should empower and compel us to live in righteousness leading to holiness.

C. Living at the Point of Biblical Tension

What was Jesus's relationship to the law? (Matthew 5:17-20)

_____

_____

The law is not to be done away with – it is not sin (Romans 7:7). Jesus fulfilled the law. With Jesus living in us, we, too, can obey the commands of the Lord.

How can we live this new life? (Galatians 2:20)

_____

_____

There is a point of biblical tension in which we must live. The midpoint is not law versus grace, but a balance between law and grace. An understanding of this paradox causes absolute dependence on the Spirit to discern God's ways in every choice of life. We are "in" the world, but not "of" the world. Justice and mercy, love and hate, or kindness and anger are choices only discernible by one in the center of God's will. God's grace has provided a new nature, by which we are now able to relate to Him and to obey Him. We must choose to rely on His provision and His life in us, to enable us to walk as He would walk.

What has this joint-life granted you? (2 Peter 1:2-4)

_____

_____

You have been given the very life of Christ to dwell in you, to empower you, and to overcome sin and the evil one.

What two actions are necessary to move the reality of this exchanged life into your everyday life? (Hebrews 11:6; Colossians 2:6-7; 1 Samuel 15:22-23)

_____

_____

Even though life's circumstances told Abraham the promise of God was impossible, he believed God. Not only did he believe Him, but his faith grew strong and he praised Him. He was fully assured in the supernatural ability of his God to do what He promised.

What did this faith lead Abraham to do? (Hebrews 11:8)

_____

_____

Faith and belief in our position in Christ will always lead us to act as Jesus did. If it does not, then it is not real faith. It is unbelief. As you begin to count on the finished work of Jesus Christ on the cross, and the power of His resurrection to be real in you, your life will be transformed.

COMPLETING OBEDIENCE

1) Memorize Romans 5:3.

2) Have you chosen to lay aside your own ability to achieve righteousness? Have you and are you continuing to count on Jesus as the absolute source of righteousness in your life? Choose now, daily, to believe in and trust on the provision of God for His transformation in your life.

3) Is there any area in your life where unbelief is evident? Why? Begin your journey of belief by praying about your need. Determine what specific action will demonstrate your faith.

CHALLENGE TWO
THE THRONE OF LIFE...
THE CROSS

"But may it never be that I should boast, except in the cross of our Lord Jesus Christ, through which the world has been crucified to me, and I to the world."

Galatians 6:14

THE TRUTH REALIZED

Paul Billheimer

Self-sacrifice is the foundation upon which the universe is built, the law by which it operates. If sacrifice were not the supreme law of the universe, would God, the Supreme Ruler of the universe, operate on that principle? Through Calvary, God is saying to us, "This is the throne of the universe, not only for Christ; it is the only pathway to power, authority, and rulership for everyone."

Destined for the Cross

EMBRACING THE TRUTH

A. Sacrifice – The Supreme Law

What law of life is expressed in John 12:24-25?

_____

_____

_____

Life comes out of death. Only as a seed goes into the ground, sacrificing itself, will it bear fruit. If the seed does not die, it will remain a single seed (1 Corinthians 15:36).

Read Matthew 27:1-66. What did Jesus endure emotionally, physically, relationally, and spiritually during His trial and crucifixion?

_____

_____

_____

_____

Jesus suffered the most rejecting, humiliating, and painful death ever experienced. Why was the cross necessary? (Colossians 1:19-22)

_____

_____

Jesus understood the law of His Father's world – self-sacrifice. He knew that through His death, it would be possible for all men to be reconciled to Him. When the mother of the sons of Zebedee came to Him to request honor for her sons, Jesus speaks of this law of life.

What does He say to her? (Matthew 20:20-28)

_____

_____

Life comes out of death, greatness out of servanthood. This is the rule of God's kingdom. God demonstrated and fulfilled His natural and spiritual law through the death and resurrection of Jesus Christ.

What does Philippians 2:5-11 affirm concerning the cross?

_____

_____

How will Jesus Christ be honored? (v. 10-11)

_____

_____

Because Jesus humbled Himself enough to the point of death, not only did He make it possible for all men to be reconciled to God, but all nations will bow in honor and worship Him.

B. The Power of the Cross

Through the cross, what did Jesus overcome? (Colossians 2:13-15; Hebrews 2:9-10, 14-18)

_____

_____

Jesus destroyed Satan's ability to enslave men to sin.

Read Matthew 4:1-11, 27:39-42. What did Satan try to get Jesus to do?

_____

_____

Why do you think the enemy taunted Jesus to compromise?

_____

_____

Satan knew the law of sacrifice. He knew that life came from death, so he tempted Jesus to exert His own power and way. What do you think would have happened if Jesus had yielded to Satan's temptations? (Hebrews 5:7-10)

_____

_____

Jesus's obedience through suffering to the point of death purchased eternal life for all who will walk the same pathway; death to self, alive to God. The cross is the power of God for man's deliverance, from a heart that is given to pleasing self. The cross is the power that breaks the dictatorship of the enemy, releasing men from the power of sin, death, and the world.

What did Paul find to be his joy in boasting?
(2 Corinthians 12:7-10; Galatians 6:14)

_____

_____

Our freedom in life will come when we, by faith, receive the power of the cross to overcome the rule of the evil one.

C. The Cost of Sacrifice

Read Luke 9:18-27. What price did Jesus tell His disciples was necessary to follow Him? (v. 23-26)

_____

_____

Write out Luke 9:23.

_____

_____

_____

What does it mean to "deny self, and take up your cross daily, to lose your life"?

_____

_____

To lose your life and take up your cross means to refuse any action or thought that originates apart from Christ, and become wholeheartedly obedient to the commands of the Lord.

Where is the new life found, replacing the old? (John 17:3; 1 John 5:12)

_____

_____

Only Jesus can produce life, because "life" is in Christ. How do we lose our life and gain His? (Galatians 2:20, 5:24-26)

_____

_____

By faith, we join Christ on the cross – dying to our own ideas and relinquishing the right to live however we want. We choose to agree with God's law of life – self-sacrifice.

Read Luke 14:25-33. What does Jesus say is necessary to walk the way of the cross?

_____

_____

We must count the cost. We must being willing to put everything aside – relationships, rights, possessions, and positions; and we must make Jesus preeminent in our heart.

What is the reward for those who are willing to pay the price? (2 Corinthians 2:14-16; John 15:14)

_____

_____

The greatest privilege of mankind is to be counted a friend of the Most High God, by being united with His heart and the ways of His kingdom. By denying ourselves, taking up our cross, and following Him, we will be exalted to the highest place – ruling and reigning with Him (2 Timothy 2:11-13).

COMPLETING OBEDIENCE

1) Memorize Galatians 6:14.

2) In order to be fully obedient to the will of God, ask the Holy Spirit to reveal any actions or thoughts that you are not sacrificing on the cross. Write them down and confess them to the Lord. Ask Him to crucify your selfish desires and fill you with His desires.

3) Speak aloud Galatians 2:20, and by faith, decree with Paul that your flesh and its desires are dead; your life is united in Christ to follow His will.

LIVING IN CHRIST...A NEW REALM

"Than which is born of the flesh is flesh, and that which is born of the Spirit is spirit."

John 3:6

THE TRUTH REALIZED

D. Martyn Lloyd-Jones

Christ was once in the realm of sin and death, He is no longer there. I was once in the realm of sin and death...Christ once entered into that realm for a while but no longer does so, in exactly the same way I no longer belong to it either; I have been taken out of it with Him because I am in Him...You and I have to "reckon" on this...It is not experiences; but the Word of God comes to us and tells us that if we are Christians at all, then, by the action of the Holy Spirit, we are in Christ. And because we are in Christ, what is true about Him in His relationship to sin and death is equally true about us in our relationship to sin and death. Therefore, I am to realize, to believe, to reckon, to hold it constantly before me, that as He died unto sin once and forever and for all, I also have done so. I am no longer in the realm of sin and death, I belong to this other realm; "alive unto God". This is not my experience but my standing, my position, my status. It is the realm in which I, myself, now live.

<u>Romans, The New Man</u>

EMBRACING THE TRUTH

A. Living in Resurrection Faith

Read Romans 6:1-4. What three momentous events identify us with Christ?

_____

_____

His death, burial, and resurrection. When we believe in Jesus Christ, we are identified, or made one with Him, in these three events. Through our faith, we actually enter into the accomplishments (effects) of His death, burial, and resurrection through the power of the Holy Spirit.

Define:

"dead to sin"

_____

"buried with Him"

_____

"raised from the dead"

_____

Are these three occurrences commands, suggestions, or statements of fact? Facts can be grounds for faith and belief. Every day, we stake our lives on believing facts. We must learn to completely believe the Word of God until our experience lines up with its truth, rather than dilute the Word to make room for our experience. Resist the temptation to disbelieve, just because you might be unable to grasp the depths and riches of His grace. Your feelings and experience will come in line with the Word when you consistently exercise faith.

When you obey, you will have understanding which will lead God to disclose Himself to you (John 14:21).

Romans 6:2-4 has three statements of fact about our believing in Jesus. What are they? Write them out again!

v. 2

_____

v. 4

_____

v. 4

_____

Read Romans 6:5-10. To what rule or power did Jesus die?

_____

_____

What does it mean to be dead to the power and rule of sin?

_____

_____

It does not mean that sin no longer exists. Sin in the world has affected the members of our body – our mind, will, and emotions. We do not have to yield to the control of sin any longer. Before salvation, we had no choice but to live under sin's control. Now, we have God-empowered rights – a capability and authority to live in righteousness.

As a man, Jesus was subjected to the temptation of sin's rule and reign over Him. Yet, He never sinned. His death was not the result of His own carnal nature or acts of sin.

By dying to the power of sin to rule and reign in His life, He rendered the enemy powerless.

Since this is true about Christ, our union with Him makes it true for us. How does this union empower us to live? (Romans 8:1-2, 9-13)

_____

_____

_____

We, too, die to the rule and reign of sin in our lives. Our very union with the resurrected Lord, a Lord who knew no sin and who overcame sin's ultimate consequence, propels us to a realm where sin has no claim on us. This truth may not, as yet, have become our daily experience. If not, it can be by accepting God's Word about our position in Christ.

B. Living in Resurrection Power

Read Romans 6:8. What does "living in resurrection power" mean?

_____

_____

We know we died with Him. We must believe, trust, and cling to this truth so that we will live with Him. The verb tense "will" deals with present tense reality. It deals with the now. We, as believers, can walk in His present resurrected life of rest, peace, and joy!

How was Christ raised from the dead? (Romans 6:4)

_____

_____

23

How does Ephesians 1:19-21 describe this glory?

_____

_____

Our union in His resurrection gives strength in His might. What did this strength and might accomplish? (Colossians 2:15)

_____

_____

In our union with Him, what are we able to do?

_____

_____

Can you imagine that the power and glory of God would not be enough to thoroughly disarm the enemy? Only our union by faith in His death, burial, and resurrection enables complete victory over a sinful, self-filled life. God is able to do exceedingly, abundantly beyond all we ask or imagine (Ephesians 3:20). This supernatural overcoming life is ours, as we receive by faith the sufficiency of Christ's finished work to meet our every need.

Read Hebrews 2:14 and Acts 2:24. What did God proclaim to all creation through the resurrection?

_____

_____

Jesus Christ overcame the power of sin and death that Satan held over all mankind. Overcoming the rule and reign of sin and the law, He purchased a life of peace with God.

How does Colossians 1:13-14 express this reality?

_____

_____

What does this mean to the life of a believer?

_____

_____

The power of sin and death has been defeated as we believe and receive the finished work of Christ. We must believe in faith that the power of sin to rule and reign in our lives has been broken. We do not have to submit to its taunting desires for control. We have a new authority in our spirit – an authority that actually gives us the desire to obey and walk with Jesus Christ. This is resurrection living!

C. Living in Resurrection Life

Paul prayed for the Ephesians to know what it meant to be one with the Spirit. What does it mean to live in resurrection life? (Ephesians 1:19-23)

_____

_____

The same power that raised Jesus from the dead is for us who believe. We can live far above demonic rulership through Christ. Through God's resurrection power, Christ has been appointed to rule over us and the Church (Colossians 2:9-10).

How does Philippians 1:21 express this empowering in our life?

_____

_____

We are no longer separate from Christ; the dividing wall has been torn down. We are made one with Him. What

was affected by Him has been affected in me. What is
His is mine; Who He is, is now in me.
Read the following verses and write out the phrase(s)
that confirm(s) this belief – the believer's life is "in
Christ."
Ephesians 1:4

_____

Ephesians 1:6

_____

2 Corinthians 2:14

_____

Colossians 2:9-10

_____

Romans 16:10

_____

Philippians 3:9

_____

These are a few of over 130 instances which refer to
oneness of the believer with the Lord Jesus Christ. The
understanding of the deeper meaning of the phrase "in
Christ" holds the key to the believer's entrance into a
new home, a new identity, and a new focus.
You are entitled to freedom from the power of sin and
death over your life. You have been transferred from the
kingdom of darkness to the kingdom of Jesus Christ
(Colossians 1:13-14). You have the very life of Christ in
you, and you have been hidden in Christ. Only as you
trust His life in you will you be able to live in the Spirit
and not in the flesh (John 3:6). Will you receive this
powerful truth and stake your life on it today?

COMPLETING OBEDIENCE

1) Memorize John 3:6.

2) Admit specifically the sin residing in your heart. You must choose to put sin away, to bury it, for you died to sin with Christ on the cross. Decide today to confess your inadequacy to live like Christ, so that He will empower you with His resurrection life.

3) Psalm 62:8 says, "Trust in Him at all times, O people; pour out your heart before Him; God is a refuge for us." Begin now to include God in your daily life by pouring out your needs to Him. Speak to Him specifically about the events in your life, believing Him to be the source of power and strength.

CHALLENGE FOUR

LIVING IN CHRIST... A NEW FREEDOM

*"I will give you a new heart and put a new spirit in you;
I will remove from you your heart of stone and give you
a heart of flesh. And I will put My Spirit in you and move
you to follow My decrees...."*

Ezekiel 36:26-27

THE TRUTH REALIZED

Ruth Paxton

*The moment a penitent sinner puts his faith in the
atoning Blood of the crucified Christ, that moment he
steps out of life, that moment he steps out of life "in
Adam" and enter into life "in Christ." Forever after he is
ensphered and environed by the Lord of Glory. He is "in
Christ Jesus" and will be through the ages upon the ages
to come. All that he is and has, he is and has "in Christ."
In God's reckoning, the believer has no life apart from
His Son. Christ is the ground in which he is rooted and
planted. Through the new birth, the believer became a
new creation with a new nature, which demanded a new
environment, a new atmosphere, as it were, where the
new life can mature into an ever-deepening conformity
to the image of Jesus Christ. This new environment is "in
Christ."*

Life on the Highest Plane

EMBRACING THE TRUTH

A. Our New Home

As a new creation in Christ, we have been raised to sit with Him in heavenly places. We are no longer bound to live as this world dictates; we are enabled to live on a higher plane. "In Christ", we are to have a new citizenship, an allegiance to a new land.

Where is our citizenship? (Philippians 3:20)

_____

_____

What does it mean to be a citizen of a country?

_____

_____

To be a citizen of a particular land means to be a benefactor of all the country has available to it. The ruling authorities of the land determine how to dispense the resources available, protect the rights of the people, and develop goals it seeks to achieve.

What is the responsibility of the citizen to his government? (Romans 13:1; Hebrews 13:17)

_____

_____

Read Hebrews 11:8-16. Abraham was looking for whom? Where? (v. 10)

_____

_____

How did Abraham pursue this city? (v. 8, 11)

_____

_____

What do verses 13-16 teach about those who walked in faith?

_____

_____

_____

What is God's response to those who walked by faith, longing for a better country?

_____

_____

By our faith in Christ, we are "raised to newness in life" (Romans 6:4), and are now hidden with Christ in God. We have a new home, a new family, and a new heritage.

As a result of our new citizenship, what two actions are we to take? (Colossians 3:1-2)

_____

_____

If you were to move to almost any other country, you would not be able to live according to the American mind-set, laws, and customs. You would need to give up those things to adapt to your new homeland. This is what the Scriptures are instructing us to do in Colossians 3:1-2. We are to stop being controlled by the things of this world and seek and think about those things that are true to our new home.

How does 1 John 2:15-17 address this change in citizenship?

_____

_____

God intends for His children to live a life in harmony with the nature of heaven!

B. Our New Identity

In the mind and heart of God, the believer is like His Son. Through the price of redemption, God identifies the believer totally with the life of His Son.

What change takes place in the believer upon faith in Christ? (Ezekiel 36:24-27)

_____

_____

What does God promise to give the believer demonstrating the authority of the exchange He has made with His children? (Ezekiel 36:28-30)

_____

_____

How does Romans 8:16-17 refer to the believer?

_____

_____

We are inhabited by Jesus Christ. Therefore, when God sees Christ, He see us; and when God sees us, He sees Jesus.

What does Galatians 4:6-7 say about this?

_____

_____

What does it mean to be an heir?

_____

_____

The American Heritage dictionary defines "heir" as "a person who inherits or is entitled by law or by the terms of a will to inherit the estate of another."

31

How would you describe Jesus's estate (His inheritance)?
(1Peter 4:12-5:11; Revelation 21:1-7, 10-22:5)

_____

_____

Since we are joint-heirs with Him, what is our
inheritance? (Romans 8:16-18)

_____

_____

Everything that was and is in the nature and life of the
Lord Jesus Christ is now "in" and "available" to the life
of the believer. The blood and life of Jesus Christ has
cleansed us, has freed us from the rule of sin, and has
empowered us with resurrection life – we are new
creations. The old has passed away, behold, all things
have become new (2 Corinthians 5:17).

C. Our New Focus

Since we have a new home and new identity, where
should our focus be? (Psalm 27:4)

_____

_____

What does it mean to seek the Lord? (John 5:30)

_____

_____

Our new focus is to seek the Lord and do what pleases
Him. We are not our own anymore (1 Corinthians
6:19-20); we are one with the Lord.

Read Psalm 84. What is the cry of the psalmist?

_____

_____

In what way are those on pilgrimage seeking God? (v. 4-7)

_____

_____

What comparison is made concerning those who seek Him? (v. 10)

_____

_____

What is the promise given to those who seek after and walk in their new identity? (v. 11-12)

_____

_____

Every believer has the privilege of living in a new home, having a new identity and a new focus. It has been purchased and given through the cross and resurrection of Jesus Christ. You must make a choice to exchange this world with its "tents of wickedness" for living in the "threshold of God." "How blessed is the man whose strength is in this, in whose heart are the highways of Zion!" (Psalm 84:5)

COMPLETING OBEDIENCE

1) Memorize Ezekiel 36:26-27.

2) Have you ever entered into identity with Jesus Christ by believing with your heart that He died for your sins? You can trust Him now by confessing your sin and believing on Him to cleanse you and deliver you from all unrighteousness.

3) Identify lusts of the flesh, lusts of the eyes, or any boastful pride of life with which you struggle. Turn from these things and submit to seeking the things that please the Lord. Make that commitment today, and tell someone about it.

CHALLENGE FIVE
THE POWER
OF HIS GRACE

"But the free gift is not like the transgression. For if by the transgression of the one the many died, much more did the grace of God and the gift by the grace of the one man, Jesus Christ, abound to the many."

Romans 5:15

THE TRUTH REALIZED

Oswald Chambers

Our Lord never patches up our natural virtues, He remakes the whole man on the inside.... Watch how God will wither up your confidence in natural virtues after sanctification, and in any power you have, until you learn to draw your life from the reservoir of the resurrection life of Jesus....It is the saddest thing to see people in the service of God depending on that which the grace of God never gave them, depending on what they have by accident or heredity. God does not build up our natural virtues and transfigure them, because our natural virtues can never come anywhere near what Jesus Christ wants. No natural love, no natural patience, no natural purity can ever come up to His demands. But as we bring every bit of our bodily life into harmony with the new life which God has put in us, He will exhibit in us the virtues that were characteristic of the Lord Jesus.

My Utmost For His Highest

35

EMBRACING THE TRUTH

A. Freed by Grace

Read Romans 8:1-4. Describe the newfound freedom received by belief in Jesus Christ.

_____

_____

_____

_____

You, as a believer in Christ, have been set free from relating to God by a set of rules and regulations. You are no longer under the wrath and condemnation of God.

What does 1 Thessalonians 5:9-10 say about God's destiny for us?

_____

_____

Since we no longer live under God's wrath, what virtues of God now govern our lives? (Romans 5:17, 20-21; 2 Timothy 1:9-10)

_____

_____

_____

_____

We are directed by grace. The purpose and grace of God through Jesus Christ destroys the rule of law, sin, and death in our lives. This is the life and immortality of which Jesus speaks.

Read Romans 12:3-21. Grace gifts have been given (v. 6). These gifts free us to live righteously (v. 10, 14, 17). How do you perceive grace to have affected your life?

What changes are taking place in your life as a result of grace?

_____

_____

_____

B. The Virtues of Grace

Grace grants favor and acceptance without expecting anything in return. God has granted us His absolute lovingkindness in exchanging the life of His Son for our sin-filled lives. Ephesians 1:7-8 reveals God's extravagant display of grace – He gives total acceptance and favor to His children.

The Greek word for grace, "charis", stands in opposition to "erga", or works. God's grace goes to the heart of man's sinfulness, restoring the repentant sinner, bringing joy, thankfulness, and life to him. Works do not achieve the righteousness of God.

Grace accomplishes virtue. How? (John 17:23)

_____

_____

How are we to "reckon", or "count" ourselves? (Romans 6:11)

_____

_____

Write out your experience of being "alive to God."

_____

_____

_____

No longer is the believer to be as one who always sins, who displeases the Lord, and who cannot overcome the trials in life. You are to see yourself as one whose spirit has come alive to the life and nature of God in Christ. It is now the desire of your heart to do His will and please Him. You may not always feel that the new spiritual nature within can overcome. Yet, the exchanged life will enable you through the Spirit of grace to know it is so!

Read Romans 8:5-11. Contrast a "mind" given to the spirit with a "mind" given over to the flesh.

"Flesh"	"Spirit"

When you are in the Spirit, an exchange in life has taken place in you by the grace of God. As you believe and trust in Christ's exchange in your nature, your experience will demonstrate the truth. This exchange in your nature is death by enslavement to sin – to a life of obedience to Christ.

Faith comes before experience. As you faithfully believe in the truth of God's Word, your life will become a life changed, empowered, and alive – because of righteousness.

C. Empowered to Live in Grace

We come first to understand the way grace is displayed in our lives. We have seen how the gift of grace brought justification (Romans 5:16). God's undeserved favor made us right in His sight. What other ways has God given grace to you?

Romans 6:14

Romans 8:28-30

1 Corinthians 3:10; 15:10

2 Corinthians 1:8-11

2 Corinthians 12:9

Philippians 4:19

God's grace in our lives accomplishes His purposes, overcomes sin, empowers for service, brings deliverance, strengthens in weakness, provides for our needs, and demonstrates the heart and source of God in every need.

39

How do we live in this grace? (Hebrews 4:16)

_____

_____

We must ask! James 4:2 teaches that we have not because we do not ask. We can humbly, boldly, and confidently come into the presence of God, asking Him often for His grace to be displayed in our life. God wants to do great and mighty things (Jeremiah 33:3).

How does 2 Timothy 2:1 encourage us?

_____

_____

How can we be strong in His grace if we are being strong in ourselves? Because of Christ's life dwelling in us, we must reckon ourselves dead to sin and become alive to God through His grace. We are now under the reign of grace to live righteous and holy lives.

"Are you foolish? Having begun by the Spirit, are you now being perfected by the flesh?" (Galatians 3:3)

COMPLETING OBEDIENCE

1) Memorize Romans 5:15.

2) Have you accepted the fact that it is only by God's grace that you have been delivered from sin? If not, count on it now by telling Him your belief in the power of His favor to overcome all rule of sin in your life (1 Timothy 1:13-14).

3) Have you reckoned yourself to be "alive with God", living totally by His grace? Ask God to display His grace in your life by strengthening you to do one of the following:
   a) Turn from habitual sin.
   b) Forgive someone you have a grievance against.
   c) Wait on the Lord to provide a specific need (name the need)
   d) Obey the Lord in ministry by serving others.

OBEDIENCE TO THE HOLY SPIRIT

"Therefore, do not let sin reign in your mortal body that you should obey its lusts, and do not go on presenting the members of your body to sin as instruments of unrighteousness; but present yourself to God as those alive from the dead, and your members as instruments of righteousness to God."

Romans 6:12-13

THE TRUTH REALIZED

John Scott
The fact that the Spirit produces [Christian character], as His 'fruit' indicates at once that there are certain conditions on which the growth depends, and for which we have to take responsibility....If the Holy Spirit is to produce good fruit in our lives, then we have to sow good seed....Yet some Christians are surprised that they are not reaping the fruit of the Spirit, although they spend a great deal of their time sowing to the flesh....By the 'sowing', the Apostle appears to be referring to the whole patterns of our thoughts and habits, our lifestyle, life-direction, and life-discipline. To sow to the flesh, he says, is to reap to 'corruption'. To sow to the Spirit, by contrast, is to reap 'eternal life', namely, a deepening fellowship with the living God now, together with that fullness of fellowship with Him which defies imagination and which awaits us on the last day.
<u>*Baptism And Fullness*</u>

EMBRACING THE TRUTH

A. Obedience to the Spirit

Read Romans 8:3-4. What two types of men are described?

_____

_____

What are the differences in their lifestyles?
(Romans 8:5-11)

_____

The believer lives according to the Spirit. How?
(Romans 8:12-13)

_____

Are you one who lives in the Spirit, or one in the flesh?
Which road have you taken? Honestly evaluate your
heart before God.

_____

_____

When the life of the believer becomes "one" or "united"
with Jesus Christ through salvation, the Holy Spirit
comes to dwell with the spirit of a man. It is the Spirit of
God living in the spirit of a man, affirming our adoption
by God (Romans 8:15-17). Not only is the believer to
possess the Spirit dwelling in him, but a true son or
daughter of God will experience the Spirit in daily
living.
What does it mean to be led by the Spirit?
(Romans 8:12-14, 13:13-14)

_____

_____

Read Galatians 5:16-26. Describe the difference in walking by the flesh and walking by the Spirit.

_____

_____

_____

The new spiritual nature of a believer desires the things of the Spirit. The enemy and our flesh may deceive you to think you do not truly desire God because your life and experience do not demonstrate that you do. The truth is, Jesus in you always desires God. By believing and acting upon your oneness with Him, His life will bear fruit in you.

Daily, we must understand and receive the full work of Jesus on our behalf, in order to obey and walk by the Spirit. It is the privilege of the believer to be changed to the likeness of Jesus Christ, by receiving the empowering of the Spirit.

B. Filled with the Spirit

Romans 6 explains the finished work of Christ, and its effect on the life through oneness with Him. Romans 8 describes the work of the Holy Spirit to affect the life of Christ in the believer.

Read Ephesians 5:15-21. How does the Spirit carry out this work in us? (v. 18)

_____

_____

We must be filled with the Spirit to be able to walk by the Spirit. How do you become filled with the Spirit?

1) How must we deal with sin in our life?

_____

_____

We are to repent and be cleansed of all unrighteousness.
Ephesians 4:30 instructs us not to _____the
Spirit. We grieve the Spirit by intentionally disobeying
the ways of the Lord. 1 Thessalonians 5:19 goes a step
further, commanding us not to _____the Spirit.
If we continue to grieve the Spirit, we will eventually put
out the Spirit's fire, the presence and power of the Spirit
in our life. We must turn from sin immediately, as
understanding and conviction strike us.

2) How do we receive the Holy Spirit? (Luke 11:9-13)

_____

_____

James 4:2-3 strongly states we have not because
_____; we do not receive because we
ask with _____

In order to be filled with the Spirit, we must desire to
obey the life of Jesus Christ and then ASK – ask for the
Spirit to fill you every day, every time anything comes in
to separate you from the power of His presence.

3) How are you to respond after asking? (Mark
11:23-24)

_____

_____

Believe that you have received! God is a rewarder to
those who diligently seek Him (Hebrews 11:6).

C. Living by the Spirit

Once filled with the Spirit, we can continue to live by the Spirit. **First,** it is important to believe the truth about your new life.

What does Romans 6:11 say we are to reckon or count on?

_____

We, in our new man, are dead to sin. Sin is not dead, but we are dead to its reign over us. We are now alive to God. We desire in our Spirit to totally please God, and are now able to do so.

Secondly, we must present ourselves to a new Master. Read Romans 6:12-13. What direction does it give?

_____

_____

What are "the members of our body"?

_____

_____

Our mind, will, emotions, eyes, ears, mouth, hands, feet, and tongue are all parts of our body we must give for the Spirit of God to control. What do you need to present for purification today?

_____

_____

Read Galatians 6:8. Summarize the truth found here in light of this lesson.

_____

_____

Hungering for the transformational work of Christ in our life enable us to set our hearts to obey the leading of the Spirit - to give ourselves totally to the governing of the Spirit, and not grieve Him in any way.

COMPLETING OBEDIENCE

1) Memorize Romans 6:12-13.

2) Evaluate your desire to obey the life of Christ. Consider the things in your life/members of your body that might separate you from the presence of the Holy Spirit. Present these things to come under the leadership of the Spirit.

3) Ask the Holy Spirit to fill you. Remember: be quick to confess sins as often as needed and to be filled afresh.

RENEWING YOUR MIND
IN CHRIST

*"Do not be conformed any longer to the pattern of the
world, but be transformed by the renewing your mind."*

Romans 12:2

THE TRUTH REALIZED

Smith Wigglesworth
*"Do you see how Jesus mastered the devil in the
wilderness? Jesus knew He was the Son of God and
Satan came along with an "if". How many times has
Satan come to you this way? He says, "After all, you may
be deceived. You know you really are not a child of
God." If the devil says you are not saved, it is a pretty
good sign that you are. When he tells you that you are
not healed, it may be taken as good evidence that the
Lord has sent His Word and healed you. The devil knows
that if he can capture your thought life, he has won a
mighty victory over you. His great business is injecting
thoughts; but if you are pure and holy, you will
constantly shrink from them. God wants us to let the
mind that was in Christ Jesus, that pure, holy, humble
mind of Christ, be in us."*

<u>*Ever Increasing Faith*</u>

EMBRACING THE TRUTH
A. A Worthy Thought Life
One of the key areas of battle for the Christian takes place in the mind. Proverbs 23:7 teaches, "As a man thinketh, so is he." Our thought life shapes our behavior. Learning to discipline ourselves in the way we think will transform our lives. One of the most needed applications of self-control is in our thinking.

What should be the pursuit of our thought life? (2 Corinthians 10:5)

_____

_____

Philippians 4:8 describes the kind of thought life we are to possess. How does this passage define a thought life "captive to the obedience of Christ?"

_____

_____

What does the Psalmist say is worthy of our meditation? (Psalm 1:2, 119:148)

_____

_____

Read Psalms 63:6. David allowed Scripture to occupy his thoughts. What was the focus of his meditation? (Psalm 143:5)

_____

_____

Where does Paul instruct us to fix our thoughts? (Colossians 3:2)

_____

_____

What does it mean to "think on things above?"

_____

Why do the Scriptures repeatedly direct us to think on
the Word of God, His character, and His works?

_____

The Word of God, His character, and His works are the
essence of life – truth, hope, and love. These are what
God intended our lives to be filled with from the
beginning. God is Holy, not willing to be yoked with
ungodliness. If Christ lives in us, we are not to be a part
of that which does not glorify and build up the life of
God in us (2 Corinthians 7:1).

Read Colossians 3:10. How is our new self to be
renewed?

_____

Read Isaiah 55:8-13. What three things do these verses
teach about the Word of the Lord?
v. 8-9

_____

v. 10-11

_____

v. 12-13

_____

God's thoughts and ways are higher than our thoughts
and ways. He has instructed us through His true Word to
elevate our thoughts to where He is – in the heavenlies.
We are to focus our thinking on absolute Truth.

In John 8:31-32, what effect does the truth have on a believer's life when he chooses to abide in the Word of God?

The Word is active, powerful, and able to discern the thoughts and intents of man (Hebrews 4:12). Meditating on truth reveals the errors of man. We naturally see the world from a fallen perspective, fixing our mind on the temporal instead of the eternal (2 Corinthians 4:18). When we are transformed in our understanding of the eternal God and His kingdom, we tightly received our personhood, others, and the circumstances of life. If we base our perceptions and understandings on anything other than the truth of God, we are fools (1 Corinthians 3:18-20).

How do we change our foolish thinking into a renewed knowledge of God?

B. Being Renewed in Knowledge
What fact is given in 1 Corinthians 2:16 as a part of this transformation?

We have the mind of Christ. What does this mean?

We have been given the Spirit who understands the things of God, and who, in turn, will reveal them to us.

51

By the Spirit of God, we can know and understand the things God has freely given us (1 Corinthians 2:9-16).

God's desire for us is to know His heart and His kingdom (Matthew 6:10). How can we live this way? (Matthew 6:9-13)

_____

_____

Jesus taught the disciples to seek His kingdom, His provision, His forgiveness, and His protection. What promise is given to those who seek God's kingdom first? (Matthew 6:33)

_____

God's kingdom is based on eternal, absolute truth. What trains us to become mature? (Hebrews 5:13-14)

_____

_____

We need solid food, the Word of righteousness. We must train ourselves to walk by the truth. What is it that needs to be trained? (Hebrews 5:14)

_____

_____

Our senses will not always give true discernment of our circumstances. They are changing from day to day. God's Word is stable and eternal. We must train our senses to judge righteously.

How did Jesus live? (John 7:24)

_____

_____

_____

Jesus judged by righteousness and truth. Evaluation is best when character is primary and those things which appear to shape us – the earthly, the outward, the sensual is secondary.

How do we know the truth? (John 8:31-32)

_____

_____

How does the truth impact life "in Christ"? (v. 32)

_____

_____

By seeking, believing, and obeying the truth of God and His Word, we are set free from the defeat and temporalness of this life. We can continuously dwell on the things that produce life – thoughts that bring us insight, understanding, and the victory of God into our everyday living.

How do we live in freedom? (2 Crinthians 10:3-5)

_____

_____

Through repentance, the speculations and reasonings of human understanding brings freedom to believe what God says. We must take our thoughts captive to obey what Jesus says about who we are, about others, and about our circumstances.

C. David's Thought Life
Read Psalm 42. What is David's response to life?
(v. 3, 5-6)

_____

_____

David honestly submits his feelings to God. He does not try to hide them. What is David's focus after declaring his need? (v. 6-8)

_____

_____

David confesses eternal truth over his situations and emotions. He speaks of God's willingness to uphold and sustain him.
David honestly responds to God. How? (v. 11)

_____

_____

He commands his mind, will, and emotions to trust God. David did not wait for his situation or his emotions to change. He submitted his earthly judgments to the authority of God, choosing to think on things above.

Are you tired of being ruled by fear, defeat, or the dullness of everyday life? Resist offering your mind over to the thinking of this world. Train your senses to obey God's words of righteousness. Be accountable to the truth.

COMPLETING OBEDIENCE

1) Memorize Romans 12:2.

2) What areas of your thought life are shutting out the knowledge of God; fear, anger, unbelief, lust, etc.? Using a concordance, look up each area and write down what God says about it. You may want to look up antonyms for the area as well.

3) Meditate on the truth you have discovered. Choose to take your thoughts captive to what Jesus says, instead of listening to your circumstances.

CHALLENGE EIGHT
SETTING YOUR AFFECTIONS
ON CHRIST

*"Oh, that their hearts will be inclined to fear me and
keep all my commands always, so that it might go well
with them and their children forever!"*

Deuteronomy 5:29

THE TRUTH REALIZED

Andrew Murray
*And so, the mind has to gather from Scripture and
understand the words which meet our needs, then pass
them on to the heart, as the only soil on which this
heavenly seed can grow. We cannot give life or growth.
Nor do we need to; it is already there. But what we can
do is to hide the word in our heart, and keep it there,
waiting for the sunshine that comes from above.
The effect of the Word on the heart is in most cases not
immediate. It needs time to take root, and grow up.
Christ's words must abide in us. We must not only, day
by day, increase our store of Bible knowledge – this is
like gathering grain in a barn; but watch over those
commands and promises that we have especially taken,
and allow them room in our heart to spread both roots
and branches. We need to know what seed we have put
in, and to cultivate a watchful but patient expectancy. In
due time, we shall reap, if we faint not.*

<u>*The Inner Life*</u>

EMBRACING THE TRUTH

A. The Old Nature of the Heart

The heart is the subject of much Scripture. What does the heart represent to you?

_____

_____

Webster's Ninth Collegiate Dictionary defines the heart as "the emotional or moral, as distinguished from the intellectual nature; affections, courage, one's innermost character, feelings, or inclinations."
It is necessary for believers to be renewed in their thinking. Also, the innermost character, feelings, and inclinations must become submitted under the rule and reign of the grace and power of the Holy Spirit.

Read Titus 2:11-14. What does the grace of God produce in the life of the believer?

_____

_____

_____

Why does man need this grace to touch and transform his life? (Mark 7:20-23)

_____

_____

Before salvation, our heart is blackened by sin, and cannot desire anything other than self. How does Jeremiah 17:9 depict the heart?

_____

_____

_____

By nature, our innermost character, feelings, and inclinations are determined to satisfy the flesh, bringing honor and glory to self. What is the root problem in darkened hearts? (Hebrews 3:16-19)

Unbelief. Apart from faith and trust in Jesus Christ, man's heart is destined to focus on the flesh and things of this temporal life. This focus will lead to destruction. God's heart is set toward those He has chosen (Deuteronomy 7:6-9). He longs for us to respond to His affection by setting our affections on Him. How can we set our affections on Him daily, when we have so many competing distractions?

B. The Rule of the New Heart
What do the following verses declare the Lord will do? Jeremiah 24:7

Ezekiel 11:18-20

Hebrews 8:6-13; How does the new covenant surpass the old?

God, through Jesus Christ, has made a new covenant with us that gives us a new heart. Our heart, filled with the Holy Spirit, has been set apart to be consumed with His character, His feelings, His inclinations, and His passions. We are no longer our own, but we have been bought with a price to glorify Him with our innermost being.

God desires to rule in our innermost being. How does His authority find its place in our lives? (Psalm 51:6)

_____

_____

Micah expresses the heart of God for his people. What does God require? (Micah 6:8)

_____

_____

Isaiah 66:2 describes one whose affection is set toward the Lord. To whom does the Lord look?

_____

_____

How does this new heart govern the life of a believer? What are its characteristics? Look up the following verses and write down what you find.
Deuteronomy 10:12-13

_____

1 Kings 3:12

_____

1 Kings 9:4-5

_____

2 Kings 22:19

_____

Psalm 24:4

_____

Psalm 112:7-8

_____

Describe God's pursuit after those whose hearts are completely His. (1 Samuel 13:14; 2 Chronicles 16:9)

_____

_____

_____

Those born again have a new heart, and are able to intimately know the Lord. Truth in the innermost being protects the desire to follow Him wholeheartedly, to be pure, wise, steadfast, secure, and fearless. God pours strength into those who passionately cultivate this new heart. Are you seeking this new kind of relationship?

C. Strengthening the Reign of the New Heart
Read Proverbs 4:23-27. What instruction are we given? (v. 23)

_____

_____

What are some specific ways we can guard our heart? (v. 24-27)

_____

_____

What causes us to turn from the Lord? (Hebrews 3:12)

_____

_____

The Israelites didn't enter into rest because they hardened their hearts toward the Lord, refusing to trust Him. We must guard our hearts from this deception. The very term, "believe", means to put our hope in all that He is. Read 2 Corinthians 6:14-18 and 7:1-2. Idolatry of the heart consumes the purposes of the living God.

God's jealousy leaves no room for sharing of affections. We choose to separate from the things God distinctly hates.

What does Paul direct us to do? (2 Corinthians 7:1)

_____

_____

Read the following verses. What wrong affections steal your passion for the Lord?

2 Corinthians 2:1

_____

Hebrews 3:13

_____

Philippians 4:6-7

_____

Hebrews 4:2, 11, 14

_____

2 Timothy 2:20-22

_____

1 John 2:15-17

_____

We choose to flee those things that do not build His heart in us. As we cleanse ourselves from those things, we become a vessel for honor, cleansed and ready for the heart of God to flow through us to a despairing world. Set your heart on God!

COMPLETING OBEDIENCE

1) Memorize Proverbs 4:23.

2) A double-minded person is unstable. Is anything competing for your affection? God is a jealous God!

3) The Word must be planted in the innermost being for truth to bear fruit. What steps are you taking to hide the Word in your heart? If necessary, seek help to devise a strategy for cultivating this new heart.

CHALLENGE NINE
YIELDING YOUR WILL
TO CHRIST

"Although He was a Son, He learned obedience from the things which He suffered. And having been made perfect, He became to all those who obey Him the source of eternal salvation."

Hebrews 5:8-9

THE TRUTH REALIZED

Dietrich Bonhoeffer

Discipleship means adherence to the person of Jesus, and therefore submission to the law of Christ which is the law of the cross.... To deny oneself is to be aware only of Christ and no more of self, to see only Him who goes before, and no more the road which is too hard for us. Once more, all that self-denial can say is, "He leads the way, keep close to Him".... To endure the cross is not a tragedy; it is the suffering which is the fruit of an exclusive allegiance to Jesus Christ.... The first Christ-suffering which every man must experience is the call to abandon the attachments of this world. It is that dying of the old man which is the result of his encounter with Christ. As we embark upon discipleship, we surrender ourselves to Christ in union with His death - we give over our lives to death. In fact, every command of Jesus is a call to die, with all our affections and lusts.

The Cost Of Discipleship

EMBRACING THE TRUTH

A. Conformity to the Image of Christ

Read Romans 8:14-29. What is creation eagerly awaiting? (v. 19)

_____

_____

What does the child of God receive at salvation? (v. 15)

_____

_____

What is God's will and purpose for His children? (v. 16-17, 28-29)

_____

_____

How will this purpose be fulfilled? (v. 17)

_____

_____

_____

Before creation, God's heart was to share His love, life, and character. He chose to create man in His image; a people who could share in His nature and respond to His love. Those who are called into relationship with God through Christ will be conformed to the likeness of His Son. All of creation is awaiting the completion of the mystery that has been hidden for ages (Ephesians 1:9-12) - Christ formed in God's children (Galatians 4:19).

The prayerful outcry of those who have received salvation is "Abba! Father!" This heart cry expresses the consciousness of one's entrance into the family of God. With this exchange of family and ownership comes a Preeminent One whom we are to follow.

Who is He? (Colossians 1:13-18)

_____

_____

_____

Read Philippians 2:3-8. Describe Christ's example of Sonship.

_____

_____

_____

_____

What was the attitude of His heart that enabled Him to go to the cross? (v. 3-4)

_____

_____

_____

What price was Jesus, as a Son, willing to pay to please His Father? (v. 8)

_____

_____

_____

Jesus was willing to die to self and fulfill His Father's plan – the redemption of man. Daily, Jesus yielded His rights to obtaining personal glory. There was a greater struggle to come – death on a cross.

What was the pattern of Jesus's life which enabled Him to endure the cross? (John 5:10, 20, 30)

_____

_____

This total dependency on His Father's leading eventually brought Jesus to a crisis point.

Read Matthew 26:36-42 and Luke 22:39-44. What was the crisis?

_____

_____

_____

_____

Jesus's humanness did not want to endure the cross, but His Spirit willed to obey the Father's plan.

How did Jesus respond to the crisis?

_____

_____

The daily crisis of the cross is choosing to yield our rights instead of holding on to selfish ambition. This is a hard and necessary choice; but the ultimate choice is giving one's life. Jesus submitted His will to the law of God – life through self-denial and death (John 12:24-25). This is the yielded life.

B. Portraits of the Yielded Life

Read 2 Kings 5:1-14. What was Naaman's initial response to the instruction of the Lord through the prophet? (V. 11-12)

_____

_____

_____

Naaman did not like the direction of the Lord through Elisha. He did not understand it, or think it was good enough for healing. His was unwilling to yield his will and trust in the Word of the Lord. In verse 13, Naaman was confronted because of his rebelliousness.

How does Naaman deal with his servant's rebuke? (v. 14)

_____

_____

_____

_____

Naaman did learn that God does not always speak the way we want or expect. To live the abundant life, we must live a yielded, obedient life, whether it is comfortable or not.

Read 2 Samuel 11, 12:1-14. Briefly paraphrase David's series of actions leading to his downfall.

_____

_____

_____

What do you think led to David's sin?

_____

_____

_____

David sinned because he chose to disregard the ways of
the Lord. He disobeyed the Father's will.

What was David's response when Nathan presented his
parable and admonished him? (v. 13)

_____

_____

_____

Learning to obey the Lord is a painful process.
Everything of our self-life must die. David, like Jesus,
learned obedience through suffering. Later, he was able
to say, " I delight to the Thy will, O Lord." Our
confession and submission to His will exceeds the
understanding of this world. We are to choose to submit
our will to His, whether or not we understand it or like it.
His ways are higher (Isaiah 55:8-9). Faith is
unexplainable and spiritual.

C. A Greater Grace

Read James 4:6. What disposition characterizes the
yielded life?

_____

Godly yieldedness brings about a disposition of humility
and grace to every situation – whether just or unjust.
God always gives a greater grace to the humble, to the

broken, and to those who tremble at His Word (Isaiah 66:2).

Describe your understanding of the phrase, "God opposes the proud."

_____

_____

_____

Pride brings resistance from the Preeminent One. The image of opposition is God "stiff-arming" the proud.

How does God respond to those who regard disobedience in their heart? (Psalm 66:18)

_____

The character of God does not allow any place for willful disobedience.

Naaman and David rejected the Word of the Lord, provoking God to oppose them in their time of need. In contrast, Jesus accepted the Word of the Lord, receiving God's grace.

COMPLETING OBEDIENCE

1) Memorize James 4:6.

2) Evaluate the attitude of your heart toward God's direction (Philippians 2:3-5). Is there anything in your life bringing the opposition of God?

3) Are you suffering in any way, justly or unjustly? How would the Lord have you respond? Humble yourself before the Lord in prayer, seeking His specific direction concerning your need (Hebrews 4:16).

CHALLENGE TEN
LIVING THE SACRED LIFE

"I urge you therefore, brethren, by the mercies of God, to present your body a living and holy sacrifice, acceptable to God, which is your spiritual service of worship."

Romans 12:1

THE TRUTH REALIZED

Miles Stanford

We will be ready to take up our cross when self becomes intolerable to us, when we begin to "hate our life" (Luke 14:26) .... The long, devastating years of abject bondage make freedom in the Lord Jesus priceless. Our attitude becomes: "I gladly and willingly take, by faith in the facts, my finished work of emancipation that was established at Calvary; I reckon myself to be dead indeed to sin, and alive unto God in Christ".... The Holy Spirit brings that finished work of death and applies it to all of the old nature, which is held in the place of death – the death of Calvary. If and when we turn from the facts and begin to rely upon anyone or anything else, including ourselves, self is released from the cross – active and enslaving as ever. Through this process, we are patiently taught to walk by faith, to maintain our attitude of reliance upon the finished work of the cross...then Christ by His Spirit...leads us as His bond-slaves (disciples), in the train of His triumph.

<u>*Principles Of Spiritual Growth*</u>

71

EMBRACING THE TRUTH

A. The Significance of Consecration

The first six chapters of Leviticus describe the laws concerning offerings. These were made to atone for sin, to signify consecration, and to give thanks. Offerings were God's way for man's sin to be covered outwardly, but they were not able to touch the root problem – man's heart. The law and the offerings could only point the way to the One who would fulfill the commandments, be the perfect, eternal sacrifice, and touch the heart.

Read Hebrews 10:1-14. What has Christ done that bulls and goats could never do?

_____

_____

Why was it necessary for Christ to die, to take away the sins of mankind? (Hebrews 9:16-22)

_____

_____

_____

God made a covenant with Abraham, allowing many to be sons and daughters in His kingdom (Genesis 15). A covenant or contract is only made effective through the death of the one who made it. Through Jesus's death and shedding blood, we are able to enter into covenant relationship with God.

The blood cleanses man of his sins. What purpose does the cross serve? (Acts 13:38-39; Romans 6:6-7; Hebrews 2:14-15)

_____

_____

The cross of Christ put to death man's enslavement to sin.

Read 2 Corinthians 4:17-18, 5:7-21. What does our oneness with Christ and the sanctifying work of the Holy Spirit compel us to do? (2 Corinthians 4:10-15, 5:7-10, 20)

_____

_____

How does Paul express this same truth to Timothy? (2 Timothy 2:20-21)

_____

_____

What did Paul obviously understand, as a result of his transformed life? (1 Peter 4:1-2)

_____

_____

Paul willingly gave himself "over to death for Jesus' sake." What motivated him to live this way? (2 Corinthians 4:17, 5:9-10)

_____

_____

Paul encountered the life-changing power of Jesus Christ through a yielded life (Acts 9). His whole being – body, soul, and spirit – were given over to the purposes of God. He saw with the eyes of his spirit, and believed there was "a glory" that far outshone the glitter of "things" in this life.

B. An Exchanged Life Loves

How did this yieldedness enable Paul to live?
(2 Corinthians 5:14-21)

_____

_____

_____

Paul was able to view others through the life of Christ. It became his passion to see others reconciled to God.

What is the greatest mark of a Christian's life?
(John 13:34-35)

_____

_____

_____

1 Corinthians 13:4-8 defines God's kind of love. For those who choose to walk the way of the exchanged life, God's love will envelope their heart, calling others to be reconciled to God. We are able to minister to others, as we receive and believe the life of Christ to be ours (John 15:5).

Read 1 John 3:11-18, 4:7-5:5. In the Greek, "to know" can be defined as "to know experientially". Contrast one who experientially knows God with the one who does not.

One who knows God   One who does not know

_____   _____

_____   _____

_____   _____

_____   _____

_____   _____

"The only thing that counts is faith expressing itself through love" (Galatians 5:6). The character of one who wholeheartedly commits to Jesus Christ is marked by faith and love. The believers respond to Christ's love by loving Him in return. This love of Christ will reproduce itself in our relationships through a disposition of faith demonstrated by love.

How did Jesus portray this kind of life? (Matthew 25:31-46)

_____

_____

_____

Sensitivity and sacrifice accompany a life given to others. An exchanged life loves others with an all-consuming passion.

C. A Living Sacrifice

Read Romans 12:1-2. Having obeyed the laws of Old Testament sacrifices, Paul understood the truth of his life, becoming a living sacrifice (Leviticus 1:6). This enabled him to receive Jesus's sacrifice for his sin, and, in turn, to offer himself fully to God.

Read Hebrews 12:28-29. What does this teach us about God?

_____

_____

_____

As we yield to God, His holy presence burns away the dross of a sinful life.

What is a disciple willing to do when he is giving himself fully to God? (Hebrews 11:8, 24-27, 32-40)

_____

_____

The life of a disciple is dependent on his obedience to the commands and call of God. The deepest desire of the disciple is to please his new master. The exchanged life is exposed to the power of the blood and the work of the cross: a cross that cleanses and sanctifies until we become a living sacrifice, holy and pleasing to the Lord.

COMPLETING OBEDIENCE

1) Memorize Romans 12:1-12.

2) Read Galatians 5:23-24. What exchange of life must you receive? Do you need self-control in light of your irresponsibility? To be good today instead of evil? To demonstrate kindness instead of harshness to your friend? You must lay your wickedness on the altar of His presence to receive cleansing, empowerment, and virtue.

3) Is there a need for you to be other-oriented rather than self-oriented? Will you give yourself to the hungry, the thirsty, the stranger, the naked, the sick? A lifestyle exchange must take place.

BOOKS

The Truth Realized in each Challenge came from the books listed below. For further knowledge on the exchanged life, we recommend you read and explore any or all of these books.

Billheimer, Paul (1983). *Destined for the cross.* Wheaton, IL: Tyndale House Publishers.

Bonhoeffer, Dietrich (1976). *The cost of discipleship.* New York, NY.: MacMillan Publishing Co.

Chambers, Oswald (1935). *My utmost for his highest.* New York, NY.: Dodd, Mead, & Co.

Lloyd-Jones, D. M. (1973). *Romans, the new man.* Grand Rapids, MI.: Zondervan Publishing House.

Murray, Andrew (1981). *The inner life.* Grand Rapids, MI.: Zondervan Publishing House.

Nee, Watchman (1981). Sit, walk, stand. Wheaton, IL.: Tyndale House Publishers.

Paxson, Ruth (1928). *Life on the highest plane.* Chicago, IL.: Moody Press.

Stanford, Miles J. (1976). *Principles of spiritual growth.*
Lincoln, NB.: Back To The Bible.

Stott, John R. W. (1971). *Baptism & fullness.* Downers
Grove, IL.: InterVarsity Press.

Wigglesworth, Smith (1971). *Ever Increasing faith.*
Springfield, MO.: Gospel Publishing House.

ABOUT THE AUTHOR

Becky Castle

Becky Castle is the Founder and Executive Director of Cornelius Connection International, a ministry with the focus of equipping the Body of Christ to advance the Gospel, establish God's presence, and build Kingdom relationships. Becky also is the Founder and Executive Director of a ministry called the Exchange, that's primary message is the revelation of the power of the Cross and resurrection. Becky has studied and walked out the Word of God in a deep way in her personal life and she has impacted the lives of countless people over the past 40 years of being in ministry. She is a gifted apostle who brings together many kinds of ministry leaders and people to advance Kingdom initiatives. Throughout the years Becky has been aligned with Chuck Pierce and Peter Wagoner at Global Spheres International. Becky currently is the leader of the apostolic center Launch Houston in Houston, Texas. She also oversees and teaches at Teleios Institute, a discipleship training school at Launch Houston. Becky has written the Challenges in Complete Obedience series to exhort the Body of Christ to press deeper into the Word of God and to experience God's fullness in a fresh way through walking out Biblical truths.

MINISTRY AND AUTHOR CONTACT INFORMATION

Becky Castle

Cornelius Connection International

2800 Antoine Dr. #2842

Houston, Tx 77092

www.corneliusconnection.net

www.launchhouston.org

**CORNELIUS
CONNECTION**
INTERNATIONAL

Series 1
Embracing the Nature of Your Father God
Series 2
Experiencing the Depth of the Exchanged Life
Series 3
Captivated By the Love of Christ
Series 4
Dwelling Behind the Veil of Holiness
Series 5
Character of Christ Within

Made in the USA
Columbia, SC
09 March 2024

32412766R00046